RECORD BOOK

Teacher

School Year Grade/Room

Reprinted 2016

HOW TO USE THE RECORD BOOK

SPECIAL PAGES

STUDENT ROSTER Wait to complete the class record until after a permanent class list is established. Complete the list in pencil, allowing for changes in students' names, addresses, and phone numbers.

BEHAVIOR AND OBSERVATION LOG Keep notes of students' behavior, both positive and negative. Write the date and the behavior observed. Also, observe students throughout the day and keep notes of things you observe them doing academically and/or socially.

PARENT CONTACT NOTES Make several copies of the Parent Contact Notes reproducible (page 10). Keep them handy to use when you need to send a note home to parents. Use the notes to convey positive messages or notify parents of concerns. You may need to send a note home to inform parents that their child has not been doing his or her class work or that the child was well behaved the entire week.

PARENT CONTACT CHECKLIST Keep track of the contact notes sent home on the Parent Contact Checklist. Use symbols to denote the reason for parent contact, such as *B* for Behavior, *H* for Homework, and *C* for Class Work. Use a minus sign (−) to denote a note sent home for negative behavior and an addition sign (+) for a note commending positive behavior.

RECORD-KEEPING TIPS

Determine the number of subjects for which you will be using the record keeper.

- Divide the book into sections according to subjects.
- Tab the book according to the subjects or periods of the day.

After establishing a permanent class list, assign each student a student number. Write each student's name next to his or her number on the desired record page.

- Color-code names by grade level if you are teaching a multiage classroom.
- If you are team teaching or your class changes throughout the day, divide the record book into sections and cut out the names columns within each section.

Determine your own grading systems using symbols, letters, or numbers for assignment and test grades.

- Color-code to differentiate between assignment and test grades.
- Use symbols for assignment completion and percentage scores for tests.
- Use the easy grader on page 64 to help determine percentages for test scores.

Record-keeping pages may be used to record skills mastered as well as assignments and tests.

- For writing skills, list skills such as *Uses Periods, Uses Caps, Writes Complete Sentences,* or *Uses Comma in Date.*
- A reading skills list might include *Knows Vowel Sounds, Recognizes Sight Words, Uses Context Clues,* or *Can Retell Story.*
- A math list might include skills such as *Fractions, Knows Basic + Facts,* or *Can Find LCD.*

Set up a system to save time with record keeping.

- Allow students to record assignments in the record book during free time.
- Assign one day per week for correcting and recording assignments and tests.
- Staple record book pages into folders to create small record keepers for each subject. Keep the folders in the area where you teach the subject.
- Keep a separate record book for homework assignments. Keep this book on hand for parent-teacher conferences.

STUDENT ROSTER

STUDENT	GUARDIAN	TELEPHONE	ADDRESS OR E-MAIL

BEHAVIOR AND OBSERVATION LOG

Name ______________________ **Date** ______________________

Notes:

Name ______________________ **Date** ______________________

Notes:

Name ______________________ **Date** ______________________

Notes:

Name ______________________ **Date** ______________________

Notes:

Name ______________________ **Date** ______________________

Notes:

BEHAVIOR AND OBSERVATION LOG

Name ______________________ **Date** ______________

Notes:

Name ______________________ **Date** ______________

Notes:

Name ______________________ **Date** ______________

Notes:

Name ______________________ **Date** ______________

Notes:

Name ______________________ **Date** ______________

Notes:

BEHAVIOR AND OBSERVATION LOG

Name ______________________ **Date** ______________________

Notes:

Name ______________________ **Date** ______________________

Notes:

Name ______________________ **Date** ______________________

Notes:

Name ______________________ **Date** ______________________

Notes:

Name ______________________ **Date** ______________________

Notes:

BEHAVIOR AND OBSERVATION LOG

Name ______________________________ **Date** ____________________

Notes:

Name ______________________________ **Date** ____________________

Notes:

Name ______________________________ **Date** ____________________

Notes:

Name ______________________________ **Date** ____________________

Notes:

Name ______________________________ **Date** ____________________

Notes:

BEHAVIOR AND OBSERVATION LOG

Name ______________________________ **Date** ______________________

Notes:

Name ______________________________ **Date** ______________________

Notes:

Name ______________________________ **Date** ______________________

Notes:

Name ______________________________ **Date** ______________________

Notes:

Name ______________________________ **Date** ______________________

Notes:

BEHAVIOR AND OBSERVATION LOG

Name ______________________________ **Date** ____________________

Notes:

Name ______________________________ **Date** ____________________

Notes:

Name ______________________________ **Date** ____________________

Notes:

Name ______________________________ **Date** ____________________

Notes:

Name ______________________________ **Date** ____________________

Notes:

Parent Contact Notes

Name ______________________ **Date** __________

____

____

____

____

____
TEACHER SIGNATURE

Parents: Please sign this note and return it to school tomorrow.

______________________ __________
PARENT SIGNATURE DATE

Parent Contact Notes

Name ______________________ **Date** __________

____

____

____

____

____
TEACHER SIGNATURE

Parents: Please sign this note and return it to school tomorrow.

______________________ __________
PARENT SIGNATURE DATE

PARENT CONTACT CHECKLIST

STUDENT NAME	B = BEHAVIOR H = HOMEWORK C = CLASS WORK																				

SUBJECT

	DATE																									
	Description of Assignment, Test, or Skill Mastered →																									
NAME																										
	1																									
	2																									
	3																									
	4																									
	5																									
	6																									
	7																									
	8																									
	9																									
	10																									
	11																									
	12																									
	13																									
	14																									
	15																									
	16																									
	17																									
	18																									
	19																									
	20																									
	21																									
	22																									
	23																									
	24																									
	25																									
	26																									
	27																									
	28																									
	29																									
	30																									

SUBJECT

																									DATE	
																									Description of Assignment, Test, or Skill Mastered ←	***NAME***
																									1	
																									2	
																									3	
																									4	
																									5	
																									6	
																									7	
																									8	
																									9	
																									10	
																									11	
																									12	
																									13	
																									14	
																									15	
																									16	
																									17	
																									18	
																									19	
																									20	
																									21	
																									22	
																									23	
																									24	
																									25	
																									26	
																									27	
																									28	
																									29	
																									30	

SUBJECT

DATE

Description of Assignment, Test, or Skill Mastered →

NAME

	1																									
	2																									
	3																									
	4																									
	5																									
	6																									
	7																									
	8																									
	9																									
	10																									
	11																									
	12																									
	13																									
	14																									
	15																									
	16																									
	17																									
	18																									
	19																									
	20																									
	21																									
	22																									
	23																									
	24																									
	25																									
	26																									
	27																									
	28																									
	29																									
	30																									

SUBJECT

																									DATE	NAME
																									Description of Assignment, Test, or Skill Mastered ←	
																									1	
																									2	
																									3	
																									4	
																									5	
																									6	
																									7	
																									8	
																									9	
																									10	
																									11	
																									12	
																									13	
																									14	
																									15	
																									16	
																									17	
																									18	
																									19	
																									20	
																									21	
																									22	
																									23	
																									24	
																									25	
																									26	
																									27	
																									28	
																									29	
																									30	

SUBJECT

NAME		DATE																								
	Description of Assignment, Test, or Skill Mastered →																									
	1																									
	2																									
	3																									
	4																									
	5																									
	6																									
	7																									
	8																									
	9																									
	10																									
	11																									
	12																									
	13																									
	14																									
	15																									
	16																									
	17																									
	18																									
	19																									
	20																									
	21																									
	22																									
	23																									
	24																									
	25																									
	26																									
	27																									
	28																									
	29																									
	30																									

SUBJECT

DATE

Description of Assignment, Test, or Skill Mastered ←

NAME

1	
2	
3	
4	
5	
6	
7	
8	
9	
10	
11	
12	
13	
14	
15	
16	
17	
18	
19	
20	
21	
22	
23	
24	
25	
26	
27	
28	
29	
30	

SUBJECT

NAME	DATE																									
	Description of Assignment, Test, or Skill Mastered →																									
	1																									
	2																									
	3																									
	4																									
	5																									
	6																									
	7																									
	8																									
	9																									
	10																									
	11																									
	12																									
	13																									
	14																									
	15																									
	16																									
	17																									
	18																									
	19																									
	20																									
	21																									
	22																									
	23																									
	24																									
	25																									
	26																									
	27																									
	28																									
	29																									
	30																									

SUBJECT

DATE

Description of Assignment, Test, or Skill Mastered ←

NAME

	NAME
1	
2	
3	
4	
5	
6	
7	
8	
9	
10	
11	
12	
13	
14	
15	
16	
17	
18	
19	
20	
21	
22	
23	
24	
25	
26	
27	
28	
29	
30	

SUBJECT

DATE

Description of Assignment, Test, or Skill Mastered →

NAME

NAME																										
	1																									
	2																									
	3																									
	4																									
	5																									
	6																									
	7																									
	8																									
	9																									
	10																									
	11																									
	12																									
	13																									
	14																									
	15																									
	16																									
	17																									
	18																									
	19																									
	20																									
	21																									
	22																									
	23																									
	24																									
	25																									
	26																									
	27																									
	28																									
	29																									
	30																									

SUBJECT

																									DATE
																									Description of Assignment, Test, or Skill Mastered ←
																									NAME
																									1
																									2
																									3
																									4
																									5
																									6
																									7
																									8
																									9
																									10
																									11
																									12
																									13
																									14
																									15
																									16
																									17
																									18
																									19
																									20
																									21
																									22
																									23
																									24
																									25
																									26
																									27
																									28
																									29
																									30

SUBJECT

	DATE																									
	Description of Assignment, Test, or Skill Mastered →																									
NAME																										
	1																									
	2																									
	3																									
	4																									
	5																									
	6																									
	7																									
	8																									
	9																									
	10																									
	11																									
	12																									
	13																									
	14																									
	15																									
	16																									
	17																									
	18																									
	19																									
	20																									
	21																									
	22																									
	23																									
	24																									
	25																									
	26																									
	27																									
	28																									
	29																									
	30																									

SUBJECT

DATE

Description of Assignment, Test, or Skill Mastered ←

NAME

1	
2	
3	
4	
5	
6	
7	
8	
9	
10	
11	
12	
13	
14	
15	
16	
17	
18	
19	
20	
21	
22	
23	
24	
25	
26	
27	
28	
29	
30	

SUBJECT

DATE

Description of Assignment, Test, or Skill Mastered →

NAME

	1																									
	2																									
	3																									
	4																									
	5																									
	6																									
	7																									
	8																									
	9																									
	10																									
	11																									
	12																									
	13																									
	14																									
	15																									
	16																									
	17																									
	18																									
	19																									
	20																									
	21																									
	22																									
	23																									
	24																									
	25																									
	26																									
	27																									
	28																									
	29																									
	30																									

SUBJECT

DATE

Description of Assignment, Test, or Skill Mastered ←

NAME

1	
2	
3	
4	
5	
6	
7	
8	
9	
10	
11	
12	
13	
14	
15	
16	
17	
18	
19	
20	
21	
22	
23	
24	
25	
26	
27	
28	
29	
30	

SUBJECT

DATE

Description of Assignment, Test, or Skill Mastered →

NAME																										
	1																									
	2																									
	3																									
	4																									
	5																									
	6																									
	7																									
	8																									
	9																									
	10																									
	11																									
	12																									
	13																									
	14																									
	15																									
	16																									
	17																									
	18																									
	19																									
	20																									
	21																									
	22																									
	23																									
	24																									
	25																									
	26																									
	27																									
	28																									
	29																									
	30																									

SUBJECT

																									DATE	
																									Description of Assignment, Test, or Skill Mastered ←	**NAME**
																									1	
																									2	
																									3	
																									4	
																									5	
																									6	
																									7	
																									8	
																									9	
																									10	
																									11	
																									12	
																									13	
																									14	
																									15	
																									16	
																									17	
																									18	
																									19	
																									20	
																									21	
																									22	
																									23	
																									24	
																									25	
																									26	
																									27	
																									28	
																									29	
																									30	

SUBJECT

	DATE																									
	Description of Assignment, Test, or Skill Mastered →																									
NAME																										
	1																									
	2																									
	3																									
	4																									
	5																									
	6																									
	7																									
	8																									
	9																									
	10																									
	11																									
	12																									
	13																									
	14																									
	15																									
	16																									
	17																									
	18																									
	19																									
	20																									
	21																									
	22																									
	23																									
	24																									
	25																									
	26																									
	27																									
	28																									
	29																									
	30																									

SUBJECT

																									DATE	
																									Description of Assignment, Test, or Skill Mastered ←	***NAME***
																									1	
																									2	
																									3	
																									4	
																									5	
																									6	
																									7	
																									8	
																									9	
																									10	
																									11	
																									12	
																									13	
																									14	
																									15	
																									16	
																									17	
																									18	
																									19	
																									20	
																									21	
																									22	
																									23	
																									24	
																									25	
																									26	
																									27	
																									28	
																									29	
																									30	

SUBJECT

DATE

Description of Assignment, Test, or Skill Mastered →

NAME

	1																									
	2																									
	3																									
	4																									
	5																									
	6																									
	7																									
	8																									
	9																									
	10																									
	11																									
	12																									
	13																									
	14																									
	15																									
	16																									
	17																									
	18																									
	19																									
	20																									
	21																									
	22																									
	23																									
	24																									
	25																									
	26																									
	27																									
	28																									
	29																									
	30																									

SUBJECT

DATE

Description of Assignment, Test, or Skill Mastered ←

NAME

																								1	
																								2	
																								3	
																								4	
																								5	
																								6	
																								7	
																								8	
																								9	
																								10	
																								11	
																								12	
																								13	
																								14	
																								15	
																								16	
																								17	
																								18	
																								19	
																								20	
																								21	
																								22	
																								23	
																								24	
																								25	
																								26	
																								27	
																								28	
																								29	
																								30	

SUBJECT

DATE

Description of Assignment, Test, or Skill Mastered →

NAME

	1																									
	2																									
	3																									
	4																									
	5																									
	6																									
	7																									
	8																									
	9																									
	10																									
	11																									
	12																									
	13																									
	14																									
	15																									
	16																									
	17																									
	18																									
	19																									
	20																									
	21																									
	22																									
	23																									
	24																									
	25																									
	26																									
	27																									
	28																									
	29																									
	30																									

SUBJECT

DATE

Description of Assignment, Test, or Skill Mastered ←

NAME

	NAME
1	
2	
3	
4	
5	
6	
7	
8	
9	
10	
11	
12	
13	
14	
15	
16	
17	
18	
19	
20	
21	
22	
23	
24	
25	
26	
27	
28	
29	
30	

SUBJECT

DATE

Description of Assignment, Test, or Skill Mastered →

NAME																										
	1																									
	2																									
	3																									
	4																									
	5																									
	6																									
	7																									
	8																									
	9																									
	10																									
	11																									
	12																									
	13																									
	14																									
	15																									
	16																									
	17																									
	18																									
	19																									
	20																									
	21																									
	22																									
	23																									
	24																									
	25																									
	26																									
	27																									
	28																									
	29																									
	30																									

SUBJECT

DATE

Description of Assignment, Test, or Skill Mastered ←

NAME

1	
2	
3	
4	
5	
6	
7	
8	
9	
10	
11	
12	
13	
14	
15	
16	
17	
18	
19	
20	
21	
22	
23	
24	
25	
26	
27	
28	
29	
30	

SUBJECT

	DATE																									
	Description of Assignment, Test, or Skill Mastered →																									
NAME																										
	1																									
	2																									
	3																									
	4																									
	5																									
	6																									
	7																									
	8																									
	9																									
	10																									
	11																									
	12																									
	13																									
	14																									
	15																									
	16																									
	17																									
	18																									
	19																									
	20																									
	21																									
	22																									
	23																									
	24																									
	25																									
	26																									
	27																									
	28																									
	29																									
	30																									

SUBJECT

																									DATE	NAME
																									Description of Assignment, Test, or Skill Mastered ←	
																									1	
																									2	
																									3	
																									4	
																									5	
																									6	
																									7	
																									8	
																									9	
																									10	
																									11	
																									12	
																									13	
																									14	
																									15	
																									16	
																									17	
																									18	
																									19	
																									20	
																									21	
																									22	
																									23	
																									24	
																									25	
																									26	
																									27	
																									28	
																									29	
																									30	

SUBJECT

DATE

Description of Assignment, Test, or Skill Mastered →

NAME

	1																									
	2																									
	3																									
	4																									
	5																									
	6																									
	7																									
	8																									
	9																									
	10																									
	11																									
	12																									
	13																									
	14																									
	15																									
	16																									
	17																									
	18																									
	19																									
	20																									
	21																									
	22																									
	23																									
	24																									
	25																									
	26																									
	27																									
	28																									
	29																									
	30																									

SUBJECT

																									DATE	
																									Description of Assignment, Test, or Skill Mastered ←	***NAME***
																									1	
																									2	
																									3	
																									4	
																									5	
																									6	
																									7	
																									8	
																									9	
																									10	
																									11	
																									12	
																									13	
																									14	
																									15	
																									16	
																									17	
																									18	
																									19	
																									20	
																									21	
																									22	
																									23	
																									24	
																									25	
																									26	
																									27	
																									28	
																									29	
																									30	

SUBJECT

DATE

Description of Assignment, Test, or Skill Mastered →

NAME																										
	1																									
	2																									
	3																									
	4																									
	5																									
	6																									
	7																									
	8																									
	9																									
	10																									
	11																									
	12																									
	13																									
	14																									
	15																									
	16																									
	17																									
	18																									
	19																									
	20																									
	21																									
	22																									
	23																									
	24																									
	25																									
	26																									
	27																									
	28																									
	29																									
	30																									

SUBJECT

NAME

																									DATE
																									Description of Assignment, Test, or Skill Mastered ←
																									1
																									2
																									3
																									4
																									5
																									6
																									7
																									8
																									9
																									10
																									11
																									12
																									13
																									14
																									15
																									16
																									17
																									18
																									19
																									20
																									21
																									22
																									23
																									24
																									25
																									26
																									27
																									28
																									29
																									30

SUBJECT

NAME																										
	DATE																									
	Description of Assignment, Test, or Skill Mastered →																									
	1																									
	2																									
	3																									
	4																									
	5																									
	6																									
	7																									
	8																									
	9																									
	10																									
	11																									
	12																									
	13																									
	14																									
	15																									
	16																									
	17																									
	18																									
	19																									
	20																									
	21																									
	22																									
	23																									
	24																									
	25																									
	26																									
	27																									
	28																									
	29																									
	30																									

SUBJECT

DATE

Description of Assignment, Test, or Skill Mastered ←

NAME

1
2
3
4
5
6
7
8
9
10
11
12
13
14
15
16
17
18
19
20
21
22
23
24
25
26
27
28
29
30

SUBJECT

DATE

Description of Assignment, Test, or Skill Mastered →

NAME

	1																									
	2																									
	3																									
	4																									
	5																									
	6																									
	7																									
	8																									
	9																									
	10																									
	11																									
	12																									
	13																									
	14																									
	15																									
	16																									
	17																									
	18																									
	19																									
	20																									
	21																									
	22																									
	23																									
	24																									
	25																									
	26																									
	27																									
	28																									
	29																									
	30																									

SUBJECT

																									DATE	
																									Description of Assignment, Test, or Skill Mastered ←	***NAME***
																									1	
																									2	
																									3	
																									4	
																									5	
																									6	
																									7	
																									8	
																									9	
																									10	
																									11	
																									12	
																									13	
																									14	
																									15	
																									16	
																									17	
																									18	
																									19	
																									20	
																									21	
																									22	
																									23	
																									24	
																									25	
																									26	
																									27	
																									28	
																									29	
																									30	

SUBJECT

DATE

Description of Assignment, Test, or Skill Mastered →

NAME																										
	1																									
	2																									
	3																									
	4																									
	5																									
	6																									
	7																									
	8																									
	9																									
	10																									
	11																									
	12																									
	13																									
	14																									
	15																									
	16																									
	17																									
	18																									
	19																									
	20																									
	21																									
	22																									
	23																									
	24																									
	25																									
	26																									
	27																									
	28																									
	29																									
	30																									

SUBJECT

DATE

Description of Assignment, Test, or Skill Mastered ←

NAME

1	
2	
3	
4	
5	
6	
7	
8	
9	
10	
11	
12	
13	
14	
15	
16	
17	
18	
19	
20	
21	
22	
23	
24	
25	
26	
27	
28	
29	
30	

SUBJECT

DATE

Description of Assignment, Test, or Skill Mastered →

NAME

	1																									
	2																									
	3																									
	4																									
	5																									
	6																									
	7																									
	8																									
	9																									
	10																									
	11																									
	12																									
	13																									
	14																									
	15																									
	16																									
	17																									
	18																									
	19																									
	20																									
	21																									
	22																									
	23																									
	24																									
	25																									
	26																									
	27																									
	28																									
	29																									
	30																									

SUBJECT

DATE

Description of Assignment, Test, or Skill Mastered ←

NAME

1	
2	
3	
4	
5	
6	
7	
8	
9	
10	
11	
12	
13	
14	
15	
16	
17	
18	
19	
20	
21	
22	
23	
24	
25	
26	
27	
28	
29	
30	

SUBJECT

DATE

Description of Assignment, Test, or Skill Mastered →

NAME																										
	1																									
	2																									
	3																									
	4																									
	5																									
	6																									
	7																									
	8																									
	9																									
	10																									
	11																									
	12																									
	13																									
	14																									
	15																									
	16																									
	17																									
	18																									
	19																									
	20																									
	21																									
	22																									
	23																									
	24																									
	25																									
	26																									
	27																									
	28																									
	29																									
	30																									

SUBJECT

DATE

Description of Assignment, Test, or Skill Mastered ←

NAME

1	
2	
3	
4	
5	
6	
7	
8	
9	
10	
11	
12	
13	
14	
15	
16	
17	
18	
19	
20	
21	
22	
23	
24	
25	
26	
27	
28	
29	
30	

SUBJECT

DATE

Description of Assignment, Test, or Skill Mastered →

NAME																										
	1																									
	2																									
	3																									
	4																									
	5																									
	6																									
	7																									
	8																									
	9																									
	10																									
	11																									
	12																									
	13																									
	14																									
	15																									
	16																									
	17																									
	18																									
	19																									
	20																									
	21																									
	22																									
	23																									
	24																									
	25																									
	26																									
	27																									
	28																									
	29																									
	30																									

SUBJECT

DATE

Description of Assignment, Test, or Skill Mastered ←

NAME

1	
2	
3	
4	
5	
6	
7	
8	
9	
10	
11	
12	
13	
14	
15	
16	
17	
18	
19	
20	
21	
22	
23	
24	
25	
26	
27	
28	
29	
30	

SUBJECT

NAME	DATE Description of Assignment, Test, or Skill Mastered →																									
	1																									
	2																									
	3																									
	4																									
	5																									
	6																									
	7																									
	8																									
	9																									
	10																									
	11																									
	12																									
	13																									
	14																									
	15																									
	16																									
	17																									
	18																									
	19																									
	20																									
	21																									
	22																									
	23																									
	24																									
	25																									
	26																									
	27																									
	28																									
	29																									
	30																									

SUBJECT

DATE

Description of Assignment, Test, or Skill Mastered ←

	NAME
1	
2	
3	
4	
5	
6	
7	
8	
9	
10	
11	
12	
13	
14	
15	
16	
17	
18	
19	
20	
21	
22	
23	
24	
25	
26	
27	
28	
29	
30	

SUBJECT

	DATE																									
	Description of Assignment, Test, or Skill Mastered →																									
NAME																										
	1																									
	2																									
	3																									
	4																									
	5																									
	6																									
	7																									
	8																									
	9																									
	10																									
	11																									
	12																									
	13																									
	14																									
	15																									
	16																									
	17																									
	18																									
	19																									
	20																									
	21																									
	22																									
	23																									
	24																									
	25																									
	26																									
	27																									
	28																									
	29																									
	30																									

SUBJECT

DATE

Description of Assignment, Test, or Skill Mastered ←

	NAME
1	
2	
3	
4	
5	
6	
7	
8	
9	
10	
11	
12	
13	
14	
15	
16	
17	
18	
19	
20	
21	
22	
23	
24	
25	
26	
27	
28	
29	
30	

SUBJECT

DATE

Description of Assignment, Test, or Skill Mastered →

NAME																										
	1																									
	2																									
	3																									
	4																									
	5																									
	6																									
	7																									
	8																									
	9																									
	10																									
	11																									
	12																									
	13																									
	14																									
	15																									
	16																									
	17																									
	18																									
	19																									
	20																									
	21																									
	22																									
	23																									
	24																									
	25																									
	26																									
	27																									
	28																									
	29																									
	30																									

SUBJECT

																									DATE	
																									Description of Assignment, Test, or Skill Mastered ←	**NAME**
																									1	
																									2	
																									3	
																									4	
																									5	
																									6	
																									7	
																									8	
																									9	
																									10	
																									11	
																									12	
																									13	
																									14	
																									15	
																									16	
																									17	
																									18	
																									19	
																									20	
																									21	
																									22	
																									23	
																									24	
																									25	
																									26	
																									27	
																									28	
																									29	
																									30	

SUBJECT

NAME																										
	DATE																									
	Description of Assignment, Test, or Skill Mastered →																									
	1																									
	2																									
	3																									
	4																									
	5																									
	6																									
	7																									
	8																									
	9																									
	10																									
	11																									
	12																									
	13																									
	14																									
	15																									
	16																									
	17																									
	18																									
	19																									
	20																									
	21																									
	22																									
	23																									
	24																									
	25																									
	26																									
	27																									
	28																									
	29																									
	30																									

SUBJECT

																									DATE
																									Description of Assignment, Test, or Skill Mastered ←
																									NAME
																									1
																									2
																									3
																									4
																									5
																									6
																									7
																									8
																									9
																									10
																									11
																									12
																									13
																									14
																									15
																									16
																									17
																									18
																									19
																									20
																									21
																									22
																									23
																									24
																									25
																									26
																									27
																									28
																									29
																									30

SUBJECT

NAME	DATE																									
	Description of Assignment, Test, or Skill Mastered →																									
	1																									
	2																									
	3																									
	4																									
	5																									
	6																									
	7																									
	8																									
	9																									
	10																									
	11																									
	12																									
	13																									
	14																									
	15																									
	16																									
	17																									
	18																									
	19																									
	20																									
	21																									
	22																									
	23																									
	24																									
	25																									
	26																									
	27																									
	28																									
	29																									
	30																									

SUBJECT

																									DATE Description of Assignment, Test, or Skill Mastered ←	***NAME***
																									1	
																									2	
																									3	
																									4	
																									5	
																									6	
																									7	
																									8	
																									9	
																									10	
																									11	
																									12	
																									13	
																									14	
																									15	
																									16	
																									17	
																									18	
																									19	
																									20	
																									21	
																									22	
																									23	
																									24	
																									25	
																									26	
																									27	
																									28	
																									29	
																									30	

PERCENTAGE CHART FOR GRADING

TOTAL NUMBER OF PROBLEMS

NUMBER INCORRECT

	6	7	8	9	10	11	12	13	14	15	16	17	18	19	20	21	22	23	24	25	26	27	28	29	30	31	32	33	34	35	36	37	38	39	40	41	42	43	44	45	46	47	48	49	50
1	83	86	88	89	90	91	92	92	93	93	94	94	94	95	95	95	95	96	96	96	96	96	96	97	97	97	97	97	97	97	97	97	97	97	98	98	98	98	98	98	98	98	98	98	98
2	67	71	75	78	80	82	83	85	86	87	88	88	89	89	90	90	91	91	92	92	92	93	93	93	93	94	94	94	94	94	94	95	95	95	95	95	95	95	95	96	96	96	96	96	96
3	50	57	63	67	70	73	75	77	79	80	81	82	83	84	85	86	86	87	88	88	88	89	89	90	90	90	91	91	91	91	92	92	92	92	93	93	93	93	93	93	93	94	94	94	94
4	33	43	50	56	60	64	67	69	71	73	75	76	78	79	80	81	82	83	83	84	85	85	86	86	87	87	88	88	88	89	89	89	89	90	90	90	90	91	91	91	91	91	92	92	92
5	17	29	38	44	50	55	58	62	64	67	69	71	72	74	75	76	77	78	79	80	81	81	82	83	83	84	84	85	85	86	86	86	87	87	88	88	88	88	89	89	89	89	90	90	90
6		14	25	33	40	45	50	54	57	60	63	65	67	68	70	71	73	74	75	76	77	78	79	79	80	81	81	82	82	83	83	84	84	85	85	85	86	86	86	87	87	87	88	88	88
7			13	22	30	36	42	46	50	53	56	59	61	63	65	67	68	70	71	72	73	74	75	76	77	77	78	79	79	80	81	81	82	82	83	83	83	84	84	84	85	85	85	86	86
8				11	20	27	33	38	43	47	50	53	56	58	60	62	64	65	67	68	69	70	71	72	73	74	75	76	76	77	78	78	79	79	80	80	81	81	82	82	83	83	83	84	84
9					10	18	25	31	36	40	44	47	50	53	55	57	59	61	63	64	65	67	68	69	70	71	72	73	74	74	75	76	76	77	78	78	79	79	80	80	80	81	81	82	82
10						9	17	23	29	33	38	41	44	47	50	52	55	57	58	60	62	63	64	66	67	68	69	70	71	71	72	73	74	74	75	76	76	77	77	78	78	79	79	80	80
11							8	15	21	27	31	35	39	42	45	48	50	52	54	56	58	59	61	62	63	65	66	67	68	69	69	70	71	72	73	73	74	74	75	76	76	77	77	78	78
12								8	14	20	25	29	33	37	40	43	45	48	50	52	54	56	57	59	60	61	63	64	65	66	67	68	68	69	70	71	71	72	73	73	74	74	75	76	76
13									7	13	19	24	28	32	35	38	41	43	46	48	50	52	54	55	57	58	59	61	62	63	64	65	66	67	68	68	69	70	70	71	72	72	73	73	74
14										7	13	18	22	26	30	33	36	39	42	44	46	48	50	52	53	55	56	58	59	60	61	62	63	64	65	66	67	67	68	69	70	70	71	71	72
15											6	12	17	21	25	29	32	35	38	40	42	44	46	48	50	52	53	55	56	57	58	59	61	62	63	63	64	65	66	67	67	68	69	69	70
16												6	11	16	20	24	27	30	33	36	38	41	43	45	47	48	50	52	53	54	56	57	58	59	60	61	62	63	64	64	65	66	67	67	68
17													6	11	15	19	23	26	29	32	35	37	39	41	43	45	47	48	50	51	53	54	55	56	58	59	60	60	61	62	63	64	65	65	66
18														5	10	14	18	22	25	28	31	33	36	38	40	42	44	45	47	49	50	51	53	54	55	56	57	58	59	60	61	62	63	63	64
19															5	10	14	17	21	24	27	30	32	34	37	39	41	42	44	46	47	49	50	51	53	54	55	56	57	58	59	60	60	61	62
20																5	9	13	17	20	23	26	29	31	33	35	38	39	41	43	44	46	47	49	50	51	52	53	55	56	57	57	58	59	60
21																	5	9	13	16	19	22	25	28	30	32	34	36	38	40	42	43	45	46	48	49	50	51	52	53	54	55	56	57	58
22																		4	8	12	15	19	21	24	27	29	31	33	35	37	39	41	42	44	45	46	48	49	50	51	52	53	54	55	56
23																			4	8	12	15	18	21	23	26	28	30	32	34	36	38	39	41	43	44	45	47	48	49	50	51	52	53	54
24																				4	8	11	14	17	20	23	25	27	29	31	33	35	37	38	40	41	43	44	45	47	48	49	50	51	52
25																					4	7	11	14	17	19	22	24	26	29	31	32	34	36	38	39	40	42	43	44	46	47	48	49	50
26																						4	7	10	13	16	19	21	24	26	28	30	32	33	35	37	38	40	41	42	43	45	46	47	48
27																							4	7	10	13	16	18	21	23	25	27	29	31	33	34	36	37	39	40	41	43	44	45	46
28																								3	7	10	13	15	18	20	22	24	26	28	30	32	33	35	36	38	39	40	42	43	44
29																									3	6	9	12	15	17	19	22	24	26	28	29	31	33	34	36	37	38	40	41	42
30																										3	6	9	12	14	17	19	21	23	25	27	29	30	32	33	35	36	38	39	40

TOTAL NUMBER OF PROBLEMS

NUMBER INCORRECT

	51	52	53	54	55	56	57	58	59	60	61	62	63	64	65	66	67	68	69	70	71	72	73	74	75	76	77	78	79	80	81	82	83	84	85	86	87	88	89	90	91	92	93	94	95
1	98	98	98	98	98	98	98	98	98	98	98	98	98	98	98	98	99	99	99	99	99	99	99	99	99	99	99	99	99	99	99	99	99	99	99	99	99	99	99	99	99	99	99	99	99
2	96	96	96	96	96	96	96	97	97	97	97	97	97	97	97	97	97	97	97	97	97	97	97	97	97	97	97	97	97	98	98	98	98	98	98	98	98	98	98	98	98	98	98	98	98
3	94	94	94	94	95	95	95	95	95	95	95	95	95	95	95	95	96	96	96	96	96	96	96	96	96	96	96	96	96	96	96	96	96	96	96	96	97	97	97	97	97	97	97	97	97
4	92	92	92	93	93	93	93	93	93	93	93	94	94	94	94	94	94	94	94	94	94	94	95	95	95	95	95	95	95	95	95	95	95	95	95	95	95	95	96	96	96	96	96	96	96
5	90	90	91	91	91	91	91	91	92	92	92	92	92	92	92	92	93	93	93	93	93	93	93	93	93	93	94	94	94	94	94	94	94	94	94	94	94	94	94	94	95	95	95	95	95
6	88	88	89	89	89	89	89	90	90	90	90	90	90	91	91	91	91	91	91	91	92	92	92	92	92	92	92	92	92	93	93	93	93	93	93	93	93	93	93	93	93	93	94	94	94
7	86	87	87	87	87	88	88	88	88	88	89	89	89	89	89	89	90	90	90	90	90	90	90	91	91	91	91	91	91	91	91	91	92	92	92	92	92	92	92	92	92	92	92	93	93
8	84	85	85	85	85	86	86	86	86	87	87	87	87	88	88	88	88	88	88	89	89	89	89	89	89	89	90	90	90	90	90	90	90	90	91	91	91	91	91	91	91	91	91	91	92
9	82	83	83	83	84	84	84	84	85	85	85	85	86	86	86	86	87	87	87	87	87	88	88	88	88	88	88	88	89	89	89	89	89	89	89	90	90	90	90	90	90	90	90	90	91
10	80	81	81	81	82	82	82	83	83	83	84	84	84	84	85	85	85	85	86	86	86	86	86	86	87	87	87	87	87	88	88	88	88	88	88	88	89	89	89	89	89	89	89	89	89
11	78	79	79	80	80	80	81	81	81	82	82	82	83	83	83	83	84	84	84	84	85	85	85	85	85	86	86	86	86	86	86	87	87	87	87	87	87	88	88	88	88	88	88	88	88
12	76	77	77	78	78	79	79	79	80	80	80	81	81	81	82	82	82	82	83	83	83	83	84	84	84	84	85	85	85	85	85	86	86	86	86	86	86	87	87	87	87	87	87	87	87
13	75	75	75	76	76	77	77	78	78	78	79	79	79	80	80	80	81	81	81	81	82	82	82	82	83	83	83	83	84	84	84	84	84	85	85	85	85	85	85	86	86	86	86	86	86
14	73	73	74	74	75	75	75	76	76	77	77	77	78	78	78	79	79	79	80	80	80	81	81	81	81	82	82	82	82	82	83	83	83	83	83	84	84	84	84	84	84	85	85	85	85
15	71	71	72	72	73	73	74	74	75	75	75	76	76	77	77	77	78	78	78	79	79	79	79	80	80	80	81	81	81	81	81	82	82	82	82	83	83	83	83	83	84	84	84	84	84
16	69	69	70	70	71	71	72	72	73	73	74	74	75	75	75	76	76	76	77	77	77	78	78	78	79	79	79	79	80	80	80	80	81	81	81	81	82	82	82	82	82	83	83	83	83
17	67	67	68	69	69	70	70	71	71	72	72	73	73	73	74	74	75	75	75	76	76	76	77	77	77	78	78	78	78	79	79	79	80	80	80	80	80	81	81	81	81	82	82	82	82
18	65	65	66	67	67	68	68	69	69	70	70	71	71	72	72	73	73	74	74	74	75	75	75	76	76	76	77	77	77	78	78	78	78	79	79	79	79	80	80	80	80	80	81	81	81
19	63	63	64	65	65	66	67	67	68	68	69	69	70	70	71	71	72	72	72	73	73	74	74	74	75	75	75	76	76	76	77	77	77	77	78	78	78	78	79	79	79	79	80	80	80
20	61	62	62	63	64	64	65	66	66	67	67	68	68	69	69	70	70	71	71	71	72	72	73	73	73	74	74	74	75	75	75	76	76	76	76	77	77	77	78	78	78	78	78	79	79
21	59	60	60	61	62	63	63	64	64	65	66	66	67	67	68	68	69	69	70	70	70	71	71	72	72	72	73	73	73	74	74	74	75	75	75	76	76	76	76	77	77	77	77	78	78
22	57	58	58	59	60	61	61	62	63	63	64	65	65	66	66	67	67	68	68	69	69	69	70	70	71	71	71	72	72	73	73	73	73	74	74	74	75	75	75	76	76	76	76	77	77
23	55	56	57	57	58	59	60	60	61	62	62	63	63	64	65	65	66	66	67	67	68	68	68	69	69	70	70	71	71	71	72	72	72	73	73	73	74	74	74	74	75	75	75	76	76
24	53	54	55	56	56	57	58	59	59	60	61	61	62	63	63	64	64	65	65	66	66	67	67	68	68	68	69	69	70	70	70	71	71	71	72	72	72	73	73	73	74	74	74	74	75
25	51	52	53	54	55	55	56	57	58	58	59	60	60	61	62	62	63	63	64	64	65	65	66	66	67	67	68	68	68	69	69	70	70	70	71	71	71	72	72	72	73	73	73	73	74
26	49	50	51	52	53	54	54	55	56	57	57	58	59	59	60	61	61	62	62	63	63	64	64	65	65	66	66	67	67	68	68	68	69	69	69	70	70	70	71	71	71	72	72	72	73
27	47	48	49	50	51	52	53	53	54	55	56	56	57	58	58	59	60	60	61	61	62	63	63	64	64	64	65	65	66	66	67	67	67	68	68	69	69	69	70	70	70	71	71	71	72
28	45	46	47	48	49	50	51	52	53	53	54	55	56	56	57	58	58	59	59	60	61	61	62	62	63	63	64	64	65	65	65	66	66	67	67	67	68	68	69	69	69	70	70	70	71
29	43	44	45	46	47	48	49	50	51	52	52	53	54	55	55	56	57	57	58	59	59	60	60	61	61	62	62	63	63	64	64	65	65	65	66	66	67	67	67	68	68	68	69	69	69
30	41	42	43	44	45	46	47	48	49	50	51	52	52	53	54	55	55	56	57	57	58	58	59	59	60	61	61	62	62	63	63	63	64	64	65	65	66	66	66	67	67	67	68	68	68